TEACHINGS OF HINDUISM

TEACHINGS OF HINDUISM

AJANTA CHAKRAVARTY

RIDER

LONDON · SYDNEY · AUCKLAND · JOHANNESBURG

1 3 5 7 9 10 8 6 4 2

First published in 1997 by Shishti Publishers, India.
This edition published in 1998 by Rider, an imprint of
Ebury Press
Random House UK Ltd
Random House
20 Vauxhall Bridge Road
London SW1V 2SA

Random House Australia (Pty) Ltd
20 Alfred Street
Milsons Point, Sydney
New South Wales, 2016 Australia

Random House New Zealand Limited
18 Poland Road, Glenfield
Auckland 10, New Zealand

Random House South Africa (Pty) Limited
Endulini, 5A Jubilee Road
Parktown 2193, South Africa

Random House UK Limited Reg. No. 954009

Papers used by Rider Books are natural, recyclable products made from
wood grown in sustainable forests.

Printed and bound in Great Britain by CPD, Wales

A CIP catalogue record for this book is available from the British Library

ISBN 0-7126-7182-X

In memory of Smt Maya Majumdar
– whose dreamchild this was!

Preface

The origin of life on earth is a contentious issue between scientists and believers. Scientists search for the truth, trying to prove its existence through rigorous experimentation, leaving no room for ambiguities. Believers, on the other hand take the existence of the Supreme Truth as granted; the rest follows thereafter with irrefutable logic.

What is generally overlooked is that between these conflicting views, there is a definite common factor about the beginning of life, the coming into existence of living matter. This is the manifestation of the 'life-force' or what has been described by many as the 'vital elan'. This force must have a 'life space' around it to provide for its sustenance and reproduction. The two must fit precisely and harmoniously for life to grow, flourish and evolve into its many different forms.

There were calamities too. The iceage, the submergences, earthquakes, tornadoes, avalanches, and the volcanic eruptions changed life space so dramatically that entire species were wiped out. There were other disasters, less dramatic but of no less magnitude. Exhaustion of natural food resources, spoiling of natural habitat, and overcrowding of life space led to large-scale disasters. The changes in environment meant that the vital elan had two options, either to adapt to the changes or be annihilated. Very often it was the latter because the species lacked the ability to adjust to the oncoming changes and reorient themselves until it was too late.

When man finally appeared on earth, he was as exposed to all the vagaries of life space as other species. But he was intelligent. He could observe, reason, deduce and apply the core of his thinking to harness the life space rather than be driven by it. He searched actively for means of enhancing the 'vital elan' and his quest was both in the physical world outside and the spiritual world within himself. The last gave rise to religion.

It is often thought that primordial man was a not-so-clever animal, who blindly worshipped the forces of nature – the rocks, trees, streams, clouds and the stars. Many have expressed doubts about organized religion on account of its being an atavistic throwback to the dark ages of the past. In today's world of fast-paced determinism, religion is often publicly scorned but privately engaged in to propitiate the very same forces that may in some way make life space more acceptable to us. And in this cauldron of conflicting desires and ambitions, the true significance of religion and the religious teachings and precepts get lost.

Man's search for tools with which to master his environment led to science. But prior to that, he had evolved language, without which no development would have been possible. Language gave him the means to communicate his thoughts, his feelings, his enquiries with others. His superior brain enabled the processing of loose, unstructured information into systematic forms. This was knowledge, the most powerful tool at his command. He could use it for harmony, growth and peace or for wanton annihilation. What he needed were guidelines for implementing his knowledge. He sought the power of wisdom. And once again, he turned, both to the forces outside to understand the mysteries of nature and within, to know the truth of his very being. He wanted to learn from the Masters who had drunk deep of the springs of wisdom and on whose teachings were founded the great religions, the pathways of discernment.

It must be noted that many religions have come into being and almost as many have disappeared without trace. They could not measure up to the changing demands of life space. Those which survived went through many trials and tribulations, each tempering its core values for greater robustness. Their Masters, often coming at the darkest hour, brought messages of hope. Of good sense. Of homespun, sensible practices which could be adopted by all, irrespective of birth and position. Unfortunately, the passage of time invariably obscured these precepts. The primary cause for this was that the language forms underwent spatial and temporal changes, restructuring and reinterpreting. These variations proceeded to filter into common usage according to their ability of easing Man's understanding. Over time, the regular languages changed their forms so radically that the scriptural languages were rendered impotent. Thus the wisdom inherent in them was lost to new generations.

This series of books attempts to rediscover and reinterpret some of the teachings from the scriptures of a few mainstream religions, in a form suitable for absorption by the twentieth century person poised on the threshold of the twenty-first. The kind of world we will make then will depend to a great extent on the wisdom that precedes every small or big decision. Perhaps the information in this book will help in reinforcing the learning for making a better and more beautiful life space for humanity at large.

TEACHINGS OF HINDUISM

Over millenia, Hinduism has emerged, grown, changed and evolved. From the hoary pre-vedic ages down to the present day, it has maintained a thread of continuity; fragile at times, very strong at others, contiuous nonetheless. It's teachings, its principles, its foundations were passed down from generation to generation, from preceptor to student by shruti and smriti, that is through recitation and memory. When writing evolved, these began to be penned down first on palm-leaf scrolls, later on paper. In different parts of the country, thinkers and teachers compiled the existing knowledge. The same philosophy was examined in different ways by different sages. The vast richness of Hindu philosophy was thus collected in the form of Vedas, Upanishads, Mimansas, Darshan, Puranas, epics and numerous surtas.

To study Vedic literature, students first had to undertake rigorous courses in grammar, etymology, astrology, phonetics and metre. Only then could they begin to fathom the intricate compositions. The time-starved, overpushed contemporary reader finds it difficult to enjoy these teachings directly. The void is sometimes filled by misconstrued and misrepresented versions by vested interests to glorify or sully Hinduism according to their personal agenda.

This volume is an attempt to present a part of the essential Vedic literature in functional terms for the contemporary reader who will be interested to note how practical, down-to-earth and socially relevant these teachings are. No ivory-tower philosophy this, but contemplation that fuels action, teachings that become food, air and light to the human nature. They are vigilantes, illuminations of the conscience to help the desirous lead pragmatic, productive and happy lives.

If you welcome a guest with an open heart,
you too will have a place in others' hearts.

Truth is eternal. So is Bliss.

May my speech be the accurate reflection of my thoughts.

May I be truthful, in thought and in words.

Sensations are the food of the mind.

The moon is the Lord of the Heart. As the moon is illumined by the Sun, so too is the heart swayed by emotions.

Work. Talking of work is not enough. Food has to be eaten. Talking of it is not enough.

If there were no Spirit, who would direct the senses? It would be like a kingdom without a king.

The world is like a river and our acts are like its ripples.

Think of yourself as a piece of wood and the word Om as another. Rub the two pieces together till they blaze in the incandescent glory of the Supreme.

As butter permeates through milk, the Spirit permeates through living matter.

O sons of eternity, hear thou the divine song of life. Know thyself.

Not just the act but the meaning of the act should be paramount.

The Supreme was there when neither earth nor water existed, nor day nor night. Believe in Him and lead a full life.

Words that can describe him do not exist.
Believe in him and be happy.

We do not have the senses that can feel him. Believe in him and relish contentment.

The sun is reflected equally in the ocean and in the pond, so is the Supreme reflected in the rich man and the poor.

Shun ceremonies and penances. Think of Om and perform your duty.

What is sin? That which your rational mind tells you is wrong.

When the sun rises over a desert, who sees it rise? But then, does it mean it has not risen?

May your heart have windows to the West and doors to the East.

Know the best to become the best.

Offer your food to the Great Omnipresent before eating.

Drink water for it sustains life.

A weak spark cannot burn a big mass. Can a weak body sustain the vast spirit?

Inherent in a tiny seed is the great banyan tree.

Would a thief threatened with death tell the truth about his misdeeds?

Erudition without conscience is useless indeed.

Starvation reduces the ability to think. So does gluttony. Eat in moderation.

Hope is better than many other states of mind.

If you destroy a live body, you are a murderer. When you destroy a dead body, who can call you a murderer? So worship life and life-sustaining forces.

The wise know neither death nor sickness.

The soul does not age though the body does.

While the spirit lives in the body, man is unaware of it. When it leaves the body, man dies.

Lead me from darkness to light.

Lead me from death to immortality.

Through knowledge, man conquers the heavens.

If you must take a vow, take it to do good.

The money that you earn from work gets spent. But the knowledge that you earn from work is yours forever.

How can you reach the pinnacle when you aim for the base?

The desire to help others is shrouded by the veil of selfishness.

The bridge between heaven and earth is made of selfless deeds.

Selfless deeds give divine insight to the morally blind.

A well-intentioned procrastinator should be inspired to take action.

Is the spirit your earthly master that it will be pleased by your physical austerities?

If your repentance be genuine like the spring that gushes from the bowels of the earth, your sins are decimated.

Sin exists in your mind. Wash it clean with the waters of true repentance.

The highway of my heart goes to many destinations, some far, some not so far, but all can traverse this highway to come unto me.

The thoughts that engross my mind determine the course of my being. As in life, so in death.

The sage speaks. You hear what you want. I hear what I want.

The eye is not the sight. It is only an instrument of sight.

Food enters the stomach but all the senses feel content.

A sweet voice alone does not make a singer.

Righteousness is the sceptre with which the weak may rule the strong.

Peaceful environs help contemplation.

He who knows is the Guru, be he rich or poor, old or young.

A wife does not love her husband for his sake but for her own sake. So with the husband.

Man does not covet wealth; he covets what wealth can give him.

The drummer's hand smites sound from the drum. But the drum thinks, "I make music."

Names are true friends. When a man dies, all except his name leave him.

If you see no road, make one to help your fellow-men.

If there is no well, dig one to quench your fellow-men's thirst.

The giver should not decide what the boon should be.

A man can live without his senses but when the spirit leaves him, he dies.

A man may hear but without knowledge he knows not what he hears.

Knowledge bereft of speech is naught but meaningless sound.

To know the meaning of words, first know the speaker.

To appreciate beauty, first understand the beholder.

The potter sees God in clay.

Who can know Him without contemplation?

Try to forsake that which disturbs the mind.

Why restrict yourself to the narrow 'I' when the whole world is yours.

When eternity is yours, what fear does death hold?

Collect wood to light the fire of knowledge.

Some take pleasure in stale food, others in fresh food. Some take pleasure in the material, others in the spiritual.

Know Him, feel Him, be one with Him.

The world of dreams is the playground of the mind.

Can you describe in words what you know not?

The body is the cradle of the would and the head its pillow.

This world is in perpetual motion. Only God is motionless.

He moves but he walks not. He is far and yet so near. He is within but appears to be without.

If you know Him as many, try to think of Him as one.

The more we know, the greater appears our ignorance.

When our eyes cannot see beyond their visual range, how can they see the Omnipresent?

As the kernel lies within the husk, so the spirit within the body.

The life force creates and the life force preserves.

Protect us, O spirit, as the mother protects her child.

Vanity is the offspring of Pride and Ego.

Knowledge without faith is like a sterile fruit.

Let your love be all-embracing like the sky.

A starving man should not be choosy about his food.

Listen well so that you can separate the cream from the milk.

When you can pray for eternal happiness, why do you clamour for transient things?

Why do you pour fuel onto ashes instead of the blazing fire?

Time is said to be the greatest force. But it is only an instrument of the Supreme's will.

Welcome the rain-bearing clouds. They bring the promise of new life.

Though we do not see Him, He sees us.

Though we do not hear Him, He hears us.

Though we doubt Him, He watches over us like a benevolent father.

In the garden of your mind, would you like to cultivate pleasant thoughts or thorny memories?

Doing one's duty blindly has limited value. It is like eating without savouring.